STOCK MARKET INVESTING
FOR BEGINNERS

Fundamentals On How To Successfully Invest
In Stocks

By

Steven Casey

Table of Contents

Introduction

You should feel richer than you do. You manage to save some money every month; you put it in the bank, and gradually, it grows. But it never seems to grow very much - the bank is paying you hardly any interest, and after a few years of saving, you still don't feel you're getting anywhere. Does that sound familiar to you? It's a problem for many people - however hard they work, however hard they save, they never seem to get any wealthier.

We're going to show you how to change things for the better. If you stop putting your money in the bank, and instead, use the stock market to invest your money in productive assets, you'll be taking on a little bit more risk but with the prospect of a greatly increased return. This book will show you how to become an educated stock market investor, able to select the best investments for increasing your wealth over the medium and long term.

I have years of experience of the stock market, both as a professional advisor and running my own personal stock portfolio. I've run my slide rule across all kinds of investments, from start-up technology companies to old-style family breweries, across Europe and in the US. Now I'll show you how to get started by making one of the best investments available to anyone - an investment in your own education.

In this book, you'll learn how the stock market works, and how to assess investment opportunities so that you can pick the good ones and pass up the dross. You'll also learn about the advantages and disadvantages of different types of collective investment, such as Exchange Traded Funds and managed funds, as well as direct investment in shares. Unlike many books on investing, this one won't push a particular method - we'll talk about a number of different styles of investing, all of which can be used with success. The important thing is finding an investment style that suits your personality and your investment objectives. In short, if you read this book and apply the lessons you've learned, you'll be well on the way to improving your investment returns and ensuring your financial security.

Back in the 1990s two young stockbrokers had fairly small bonuses to invest. One bought a red Ferrari and put a down payment on a large house in a chic neighborhood. The other put most of the money into funds in emerging markets - at the time considered quite an aggressive move. The first analyst is still paying down debt. The second became financially independent in her forties, and was able to take two years as a sabbatical to travel around the world. Which would you rather be - the guy with the Ferrari, or footloose and fancy free?

You might not have much of a bonus to invest. But investing regular small amounts can make a huge difference to your financial prospects. One young graduate decided as soon as he got a job to start saving five percent of his monthly income, and put it into shares he'd picked for their long term growth prospects. When he received dividends, he invested them instead of spending the cash. Ten years later, he was looking at more than double what he'd started with.

This book can change your life. Instead of putting your money in the bank and getting a slow drip of derisory interest on your cash, you can invest in high quality shares and receive both dividend income and price appreciation. You might be putting money aside for any number of reasons - to fund retirement, or a sabbatical, or to create investment income that can help support a better lifestyle for you and your family.

But you should get started right now. "Time is money" - quite literally, because of the power of compounding. If you make an extra four percent return this year (and that's quite low - historically, equity returns have usually been around 7-8%), next year you'll earn money on your original investment, and on that extra four percent too. Over ten years, that's an extra 48 percent. But of course, the longer you wait, the less of that extra return you'll make - that's why it's important to start as soon as you're able to.

Make your first step towards a wealthier and more secure future by buying this book, and learning how to invest wisely.

Chapter 1: The basics of stock market investment

You're probably keen to start learning how to value investments and build your portfolio. But before we start, we need to make sure you understand the basics of stock market investment; what you're actually buying, and how markets work. Of course, you might know this already - but it may still be worth a quick refresher course before we wade into the efficient market theory, methods of analyzing returns on capital, and momentum investing.

Let's start by looking at what you're actually buying when you buy shares.

1.1 Corporate structure and equity issues

Although an individual person can run a business, or any number of people can join a partnership, most large businesses are run as limited companies. A company acts as a single entity (a single 'legal person'), but its capital is divided into a number of shares, which can be held by individuals or companies, or by institutional investors such as mutual funds or pension funds.

When you buy a share, you're buying a small proportion of the company's assets and earnings. But you're not actually buying the assets - the company owns its office, and the tables and chairs; you own a proportion of the company, not one chair or half a table. You're also buying a vote on major decisions, such as whether to accept a takeover bid, or to change auditors, though you're not involved in the actual management of the company. (Some major shareholders are able to exert significant influence over company strategy, and of course, some directors and managers of companies are also significant shareholders - but the roles of shareholders and directors are legally distinct.

You're also buying a share in a *limited liability* company. That means you can only lose your original investment - no one can come after you for more. If a company loses a massive lawsuit, the worst that can happen is that it goes bust, and your shares are worth nothing; no one has a claim on your house or bank balance.

As an investor you're going to be looking quite hard at what your percentage of the business delivers in earnings, and in cash (in the form of dividends). If, let's say, the company makes $35,000 in post-tax profit, then your share of that is $1,750. It's very unlikely that you'll receive all that as cash, and indeed you might not get any payout at all, but that's *theoretically* your money. It's usually expressed as earnings per share (EPS), a standardized figure that is shown in the annual report of the company.

A company can always issue new shares. That can have various effects, depending on the price for which the new shares are issued. If they are issued at a lower price than the market price, that could reduce the size of the stake you have in the company.

Suppose you buy 5 shares in a company that has 100 shares in total, at $1000 each; your shares are worth $5000 out of a total value for the whole company of $100,000. That total value is what we call *market capitalization.*

The company may now decide that it wants to invest in a new production technique that requires $9,000 worth of new machinery to be installed. To pay for the new plant, it issues shares to a friendly large investor; to reward him for backing the new initiative, the company issues the shares at a discount to the market price, so that he gets his shares for just $900 each. So he's got ten shares for the price of nine.

You may not think that's a problem. Surely the price he paid doesn't matter? But let's look at what happens to the value of the company. It now has 110 shares in issue, but they are worth $109,000 - the original $100,000 plus the $9,000 of new capital. Divide that by 110, and you get $990 a share - so you've lost $10 a share, or $50 overall. You'd better hope that new plant makes enough money to pay you back for the *dilution* - that is, the reduction in value of your shares when new shares are issued at a discount.

Fortunately, there are a number of rules that most stock exchanges apply to share issues made at a discount, in order to protect the rules of existing shareholders. Of course, if you have the chance to buy shares at a discount yourself, when a company in which you own shares has a new issue of equity, it can be well worth your while.

1.2 Dividends and earnings

Earnings per share is your theoretical return on investment and it's the figure that appears on the front of every analyst's research note and by which companies' values are judged. But you will also need to think about dividends, which are your tangible return - the cash that is distributed to shareholders at the end of the year, and which you'll actually receive in your bank account. Earnings, if you like, represent the total food in the fridge. Dividends are what you get to eat today. You wouldn't, normally, try to eat everything that's in the fridge at one go, and in the same way most companies, in normal circumstances, wouldn't distribute all of their earnings; some money will be kept back for investment in the business, or perhaps to help pay down debt.

Depending on your investment objectives and style, dividends can make up an important part of your investment return. That's particularly the case over the long term, if you reinvest dividends, as the magic of compounding (which we already talked about in the introduction) will work on your behalf. Some companies, and some brokers, provide automatic reinvestment schemes such as DRIPS (Dividend Re-Investment Program). This can be a great way to simplify your life and make that reinvestment automatic.

Dividends are in some ways similar to interest on a fixed rate account, or to the coupon on bonds. But in one way, they are very different - while a coupon is fixed, dividends can grow over time as the company increases its profits. This makes income investment in equities a remarkably good way to increase your wealth, as not only do you get the effect of compounding, you get growth as well.

1.3 Risk and return

You may hear from friends you tell about your plans that stock market investing is 'risky'. Well, it is - but then life is risky.

Actually, the word 'risky' isn't very helpful, because as an investor, you need to think about risk as a spectrum, from a sure thing (like keeping money in the bank and getting the rate of interest you signed up for) to a very high risk (like an early stage disruptive technology company). You need to be able to evaluate and quantify risk.

Risk has a twin brother, return. Risk and return are like Siamese twins - they are intimately joined. Generally, the higher the risk you run, the higher the return you'll make if successful. To be a successful investor, you need to think both about the kind of risk you're prepared to run, and about the kind of return that you want to achieve. For instance, if you're in your thirties and making good money in your job, you might say;

- "I want to achieve returns significantly higher than the market to achieve long term capital growth," and

- "I am happy to run the risk of losing 100% of any individual investment, but I'll limit each investment to 10% of my portfolio."

An investor who doesn't have so much money coming in or is close to retirement, so he'd find it difficult to make up any losses, might want to limit any losses to 10% of any investment - but then he would also have to accept that his returns might be lower.

The risk/reward ratio can be skewed. Some investments have high rewards but the risks are less than most people think - these are great investments. Other investments have low rewards and high risks, and you need to avoid these - often, they're complex, and they are being touted by financial advisers and banks. Many investors simply don't do enough research to find out where the risks really lie. For instance, mortgage-backed securities turned out to be much less safe than investors had been told in the sub-prime mortgage crisis of 2007-8. In fact, credit quality had been declining, increasing the risk of defaults, but you had to look hard at the small print in the prospectuses to find out. 'Precipice bonds' were sold as income investments to investors who needed a good yield, but no one explained the fact that the capital invested in the bond was at very high risk.

The successful investor is not one who either embraces risk, or who avoids it - what determines success is taking an educated attitude and always looking at the risk/reward ratio to makes sure the odds are in your favor.

By the way, don't ever be lazy about evaluating risk. Financial advisors often tell you that investing in bonds is less risky than investing in equities. They rarely point out that the returns are lower. But also, after years of very low bond yields, bonds are extremely highly valued; when interest rates rise, bond prices go down. That, in our book, is a situation that makes bonds high risk right now, although that's not usually the case. Always think through the risks yourself - it's your money, after all!

1.4 Stock markets and investor behavior

Finally, let's take a look at how stock markets work. Many investors get stuck on the pure mechanics, but the most successful investors understand that stock markets are driven by human psychology.

The stock market is a *secondary market*. With the exception of Initial Public Offerings (IPOs) when a company raises new funds, you'll be buying 'pre-loved' shares. Every transaction needs one investor to sell and another to buy, though market-makers or specialists provide a buffer in the middle. Market-makers take a risk by holding inventory, so they make their money through the 'spread' - the difference between the price at which they buy shares ('bid price') and the price at which they sell ('offer price'). Market-makers offer firm bid and offer prices, which means even if they can't match your sell order of 100 Intel shares with a buyer right now, you're still going to be able to sell, and they'll take the stock on their books till they find a buyer. (Watch out though; prices are only firm at a given level - say for 100 or 400 shares - 'price and size'.

Market-makers set the price and the spread to reflect the supply and demand that they experience. If everyone is trying to sell Intel shares, then they'll reduce their prices. It's a simple market mechanism, but since it's driven by investor psychology, it can sometimes work in irrational ways. Two big emotions drive a lot of investing - greed and fear; unsurprisingly, such strong emotions can overcome investors' reason. So the market often behaves like a piece of elastic; it will stretch, and stretch, and stretch, and then suddenly spring back violently. Investors get over-optimistic, as happened in the late 1990s with technology stocks, and push share prices higher and higher till valuations are stretched - and then when things go wrong, the market over-reacts savagely.

That's one reason you should never try to buy exactly at the bottom and get out exactly at the top. If you get out when valuations are high enough to be a concern, and when the market is over-optimistic, you may be leaving 10 percent gains on the table for someone else; but if you wait till what you think is the top, markets could fall very suddenly and very fast, so that by selling too late, you'll actually lose more.

Herd behavior is built into human psychology, and that makes many investors follow the market without challenging the prevailing view. If you watch the film *The Big Short* (or read the book) you'll see how many times analysts and fund managers who questioned the valuation of sub-prime mortgage securities were ignored - because they were going against the 'herd'. You might also want to remember that native Americans used to use herd mentality to hunt buffalo by driving huge flocks over the edge of a cliff - that's what happens to the stock market. By the time investors realize that there's only air in front of them, it's too late - the market has fallen over the edge!

Fashion also plays a part in the market. Certain sectors become fashionable, often for a very good reason - for instance, technology became so highly valued because tech companies were growing very fast and getting huge economies of scale. Unfortunately, investors tend to back the trend long after the original reason for investing no longer applies.

Big opportunities for investors often come in areas of the market that are highly unfashionable and have practically been forgotten. For instance, by 2003 investors could buy highly profitable tech companies in areas such as consulting, CAD/CAM, Enterprise Management Systems and accounting, for ridiculously low valuations; Sage, SAP and Oracle were cheaper to buy than high street restaurants at one point.

1.5 Check your own mindset

Self-knowledge is one of the factors that differentiates really successful investors from the also-rans - if you are aware when basic human instincts are pushing you in a particular direction, you'll be able to stop yourself making some very basic investment mistakes.

- **Confirmation bias** - we tend to look for and remember information that confirms our views, and ignore or avoid information that challenges them. Instead, go out of your way to play devil's advocate and find all the best arguments against your investment; then if you still think you're right, you probably are.

- **Anchoring** - investors often get fixated on a particular number. For instance, if they start off valuing a stock at $50, they'll remember that $50 even if the company's fundamentals change in a way that makes it worth much more, or much less. Anchoring can make you miss really good investments, where a 'dog' of a company starts turning itself around, so try to avoid it.

- **Hindsight bias and overconfidence** can limit your ability to learn from your trades. Look at both losing bets and successful investments and ask yourself; "How much of what I did was luck? What did I know at the time? Was there information I could have known but didn't? And did I make the best decision with the information that was available to me at the time?" This will stop you getting overconfident, but it will also show you any shortcomings in your investment process so that you can address them next time round.

- **loss aversion** makes many investors behave sub-optimally. We tend to get fixated on avoiding losses rather than focusing on making gains. That can lead to very bad investment decisions. Be aware of any tendency to loss aversion, and always do the math on expected outcomes - don't rely on instinct.

- **Disposition effect** is similar to loss aversion - many investors limit their success by selling their most successful investments ('taking profits') and keeping losers. To avoid disposition effect, look at valuations and risk when you're taking sale decisions - don't look at your in-price.

Chapter 2: What is a share really worth? Valuation ratios

One of the factors that divides the successful investor from the also-rans and the amateurs is a good grasp of company valuation. When you hear people talking about stocks, though, they rarely seem to talk about values. You hear them say "Amazon shares are going up," or "Amazon is growing really fast," or "SaaS is going to be a huge trend, so Salesforce is a buy" - but taxi drivers never tip you a stock because it's thirty percent undervalued. So they're probably not going to read this chapter - but you are, and getting a grasp of these basic principles will make you a wiser, smarter, better and more successful investor.

2.1 The efficient market theory

The stock market is a wonderful organism. Through the various participants in the market - analysts, traders, company officers, individual investors - it gets to hear pretty much everything that's going on, and like some kind of big slow-moving creature it gradually chews and digests that information and adjusts the prices of investments accordingly.

The efficient market theory says that share prices always fully reflect the sum total of information available to the market. A direct implication is that it's impossible to beat the market consistently, since stocks always trade at their fair value. The theory also implies that future prices can't be predicted by analyzing past data - that prices respond only to new information.

However, increasing numbers of researchers have criticized this theory. For instance, there's evidence that there is a real momentum effect, so that stocks which have done well for the last 12 months will probably continue to do so for the next 12 months too. Behavioral economists point to the ways that cognitive biases and errors in reasoning lead many investors to make poor investment decisions, allowing more rational investors to profit from bargains in neglected stocks.

None the less, the efficient market theory should prove a useful antidote to hubris - as well as a steer to good investment practice. You won't beat the market by knowing more stuff or having more accurate forecasts - unless, of course, you're trading on price-sensitive information (which is a crime in most jurisdictions) - but you *can,* at least if you believe the behavioral economists, beat the market by being disciplined, rational, and hard-working.

2.2 The price-earnings ratio

The price-earnings ratio or PER is the number every analyst highlights at the top of their research notes. It's the one comparable that lets you analyze pretty much any company (except, perhaps, REITs and finance companies) and rank it vis-a-vis others. It's basic to the way the stock market assesses investments, and if you've ever seen what happens to a big stock that comes out with a surprise earnings downgrade, you'll know just how much the PER tail can wag the market capitalization dog.

Earnings per share is a simple concept. Take the company's profit after paying interest and tax, and divide by the average number of shares in issue. (You use the average number because shares issued part way through the year are only entitled to the proportion of the earnings that was made after they were issued.) Of course the devil is in the detail, so expect to do a fair amount of reading through the notes to the company's accounts so that you can adjust for non-recurring items, for instance. (We won't go into the accounting treatments; accounting standards are an ever-moving goalpost, and if you want to get technical, you need to find a good book on current accounting practice. What you're looking for as an investor isn't accounting accuracy, but a number that you think is robust and represents the real profit generating capability of the business.)

And the price/earnings ratio is quite simply the share price divided by earnings per share. It shows how much you're willing to pay for each dollar of earnings. You'll pay a multiple for two reasons;

1. the company will continue to generate profits way into the future, so you're not just buying this year's earnings, you're buying a continuous income stream;

2. you would generally expect those earnings to grow, over time - that's one of the main reasons for investing in equity rather than putting your money in the bank.

If you turn the PER calculation around and instead calculate earnings as a percentage of the share price, you have what's called the *earnings yield*. So a company with $3 earnings and a share price of $39 has a PER of 39/3 = 13, which can also be expressed as an earnings yield of 3/39x100 = 7.7%. That can be compared with yields on other investments such as bonds (2.8%) or commercial property (7-8%), though remember, earnings is your theoretical return, not the actual money you get in dividends.

Obviously the PER isn't very useful in itself, but it's a great yardstick for comparing companies. However, it's not as easy as simply buying the lowest rated (= lowest PER) stock in a sector. There are a number of other factors you'll want to consider.

- First and foremost, you have to work out whether the low-rated company deserves to be poorly rated. Perhaps it has out-of-date products, poor management, or high debt and low margins. The PER should reflect the quality of the business. Of course, if it doesn't, you may have found a bargain.

- You need to look at forward as well as historical PERs. Sometimes, a stock has what looks like a ridiculously high historical PER but is selling at quite a reasonable forward rating. That can happen where an early stage company is just beginning to make profits, or where a loss-making company has been turned around - earnings will increase dramatically for a couple of years. In this case it's generally the forward PER that you should trust - but you should be convinced that it will actually be achieved.

- Look at the range of PERs for the sector. Is it very wide, reflecting a wide dispersion of growth trends and profitability, or is it fairly narrow with maybe just a couple of outliers?

- Look at the PER for the market as a whole. How do the stock and sector you're looking at relate to the overall market? Do you think the market has got it right? (Remember, we're saying the market *isn't* always efficient.)

- Look at historical levels of PER multiples. You can get a 90 year chart of the S&P 500 PER, so you can see what are the highest and lowest levels the market has ever been and how today's valuations compare. Higher valuation levels generally correspond with lower future financial returns - but you need to bear in mind that different eras had different levels of inflation and interest rates.

- The CAPE or Schiller ratio is based on the average inflation-adjusted earnings of the last ten years for the S&P 500. You won't find a CAPE ratio for individual stocks, but it's available for a large number of stock markets worldwide. It's useful as giving you an average that smooths out short-term blips and lets you see how highly the market is valued compared to historical levels.

So for instance, let's look at AbbVie (ABBV), a pharmaceutical company that's trading on 24 times earnings. Earnings are growing at 20% or so, so that would come down to a PER of 20 next year. If you compare the sector average of 46.4 current and 23.9 forecast, AbbVie looks cheap. The PER on the S&P 500 is 24.18, and there are a whole load of stocks in the index that aren't showing anything like 20% annual growth, so again, AbbVie looks inexpensive. We don't have enough yet to justify a purchase decision - but those ratios are certainly enough to justify doing some more research on the stock with a view to buying it if the story stacks up.

One refinement of the PER that can help you assess growth stocks is the Price Earnings / Growth ratio, or PEG. It's easy to calculate - taking the AbbVie numbers we already cited, it's 20 (earnings) divided by 20 (percentage growth) = 1.0. A company that's rated on only 12 times earnings but is growing at 20% would have a PEG of 0.6. A PEG of 1 shows that the company is fairly valued with regard to its growth prospects, while a PEG of less than 1 shows that it's undervalued. The PEG isn't an absolute value, and the concept has been criticized by some academics as being vastly oversimplified, but it can give you a ballpark feel for where the current valuation is pitched.

2.3 EBITDA multiples

A problem with earnings based multiples is that they include a number of non-cash items as well as including interest payments. Imagine two companies that have the same level of sales, the same operating profit margin, and the same tax rate. They should have the same earnings, right? But if one of them is mainly funded by equity, and the other one has a pile of debt, the earnings will be different - the debt-funded company will have a big interest bill to pay. Equally, even if they had the same financing, they might show different earnings because the accountants at one company had decided to write off plant and machinery in ten years, and the other company used a fifteen year depreciation policy.

Looking at EBITDA multiples evens out these effects.

Most financial stats sites as well as annual reports now show EBITDA figures, but they're fairly easy to calculate from an annual report - you take EBIT (operating profit, before interest and tax) and add back depreciation and amortization. (The whole idea of depreciation is to spread the cost of equipment over the years in which it's in use. For instance, if you buy a car for $20,000 and use it for ten years, then an accountant says that you're really paying $2,000 a year for it. But in fact, if you bought the car with cash, you know that next year, you won't be paying anything for it at all.)

We can either calculate a price to EBITDA ratio along exactly the same lines as the PER, or we can use another concept - enterprise value (EV). While the market capitalization. of a company represents the value of all its shares in issue, the enterprise value is the market capitalization. plus any debt financing - the total funds available to the company. Again, the idea is to strip out differences in financing between companies to make the figures more comparable.

EBITDA multiples are a bit lower than PERs. For instance, the pharmaceutical sector is trading on an EV/EBITDA of 14.45, quite a bit lower than the historic PER of 46.4.

EBITDA multiples are particularly useful for companies that have high financing costs and high depreciation on recent investments, or which are unprofitable on a post-tax basis. For instance, EBITDA has traditionally been used for valuing cable TV, telecoms and technology companies that have invested heavily in their networks but aren't yet profitable, or have very low earnings owing to their early stage of development.

2.4 Free cash flow multiples

Even once we've adjusted post-tax profit to EBITDA, that doesn't reflect all the cash movement that occurs in a business. A company that is investing heavily in bringing its obsolescent manufacturing plant up to date, and another that has fully up-to-date plant and consequently fairly low investment, might have the same earnings - but one of the businesses is generating a lot more cash than the other.

That's where free cash flow (FCF) multiples come in. To get free cash flow, we need to do quite a few adjustments to the net income. This can be time-consuming but it's well worth your time. The table below shows how it works.

Net income $000	300
Add back depreciation and amortization	200
	500
Now subtract working capital changes:	
Increase in inventories	-60
Increase in receivables	-200
Increase in payables	+70
Operating cash flow =	310
Subtract investment in long term assets	-300
Free cash flow =	10

When a company is growing fast, if it has to extend credit to customers, it can find that a large amount of cash is tied up in this way. Here, you see that there's an increase in receivables of $200,000 - that might reflect the start of a big export contract. Inventories might also soak up cash. The business can of course rely on credit extended by suppliers to help it - but this company hasn't been particularly successful in doing so with only $70,000 of supplier credit. Working capital can be a huge swing factor, and relatively few investors do this calculation - so this is one of your chances to beat the market.

A big export contract might also mean having to invest in new equipment to meet the special demands of that market, such as particular packaging requirements. This company has a chunky $300,000 of capital expenditure to report. So although the company has what looks like a healthy net profit of $300,000, its free cash flow is a puny $10,000.

How you'd approach this as an investor depends on the other information you find out about the company. If this is a one-off, and the big bet on the export contract opens up a whole new market in the long term, this could be a great investment. But if the company seems to have poor cash flow every year, it could be "buying its profits" - and never end up generating significant amounts of cash.

Once you have the FCF figure for the company, it's easy to calculate either Price / FCF (dividing the total market capitalization. of the company by the total cash flow) or EV / FCF. Like PERs and EBITDA multiples, it's a comparative measure, enabling you to check on the cash generative properties of comparable companies. It is, really, quite a lot of work, so be prepared to spend a while with a spreadsheet and some downloads of company accounts - but it can be very well worth while, as the case study below shows.

Case study: A disaster waiting to happen

In 1992 Guinness Peat Aviation decided to hold an
IPO. It was the world's biggest lessor of airplanes,
with over a third of the market. Airlines couldn't
afford the huge cost of new planes from their
depleted resources, but GPA let them lease rather
than buy - a cost-effective way to refresh their fleets.
GPA was growing fast, and it had pretty much
locked up advance orders from Airbus and Boeing,
at great prices because of its massive purchasing
power.

What could possibly go wrong?

One analyst decided to go through the cash flow
account. While the company appeared to make
good net income, free cash flow was small or
negative. GPA was spending more on new planes
than it was making in lease payments, and it looked
as if that would be the case for the foreseeable

future. That's partly down to the cash flow characteristics of asset leasing companies (as well as real estate companies) - a big upfront capital payment followed by a long period of smaller rental returns - but because GPA was growing so strongly, the pattern was accentuated.

The deciding factor for this analyst was a small note in the accounts that GPA had subscribed to shares in one airline. That airline was also a significant customer. So the profits looked great - but the cash flow account told the full story. Based on the analyst's report, their bank decided not to take part in the IPO. Others followed suit, and the IPO collapsed at the last moment. The company plunged into a crisis and by 1993 had to undergo a restructuring giving GE Capital operational management of its fleet and an option to buy the whole business.

2.5 Dividend yield

Dividend yield is the easiest of all the valuation methods to calculate. It's quite simply the dividend as a percentage of the share price. This is the cash return on your shares, so if you're investing for income, it will show you how much better off you'll be *this year* than leaving the money in the bank. (Of course, some companies don't pay dividends at all, and others only very low dividends; but in many cases, you'll be substantially better off.)

Microsoft, for instance, has a 1.9% yield, and Apple 1.6%. Most US banks are paying less than 0.1% on deposit accounts, though with five year CDs you can get up to 2.6%. The big question: do you think Apple and Microsoft can grow their dividends and their business? Or is the risk-free, but nil-growth, CD a better bet?

Watch out for companies that are paying special dividends, sometimes because they've sold off a subsidiary or are paying away cash that is excess to business requirements. For instance, Facebook paid a special dividend to class C shareholders in 2016 - but that's unlikely to be repeated. Valuing Facebook stock on a dividend yield basis would have been wrong, as it implies you expect the dividend to be repeated, whereas it was just a one-off.

Don't forget that the dividend yield is only one element of the total return to you as an investor. You will also benefit from any increase in the capital value of the shares. Obviously you do also run a higher risk with your capital than putting it in a CD or deposit account, but the good news for you as an investor is that over time, equity returns have comfortably beaten the returns on interest-bearing accounts.

2.6 Book value

Book value is the value of the company's assets. To be accurate, we should explain that it's the *accounting* value of the company's assets, based on the historical price paid, minus depreciation over the relevant period. That could be very different from the *market* value of the assets. For instance real estate might be represented at a value which significantly undervalues it. If you had bought a commercial building in New York twenty years ago, it would now be worth *less* in the books than when you bought it. That's clearly not up with events. Assets can be revalued if a business is acquired, but generally, not otherwise.

Price to book value is very simple to calculate using the share price divided by the net asset value per share (or market capitalization. divided by net assets).

Given the caveat about accounting values versus real values, you might think price to book value is useless as a valuation technique. However, if you're hunting for deep value shares, sometimes it can alert you to a major undervaluation. It's very useful as a screening tool, because almost all financial information sites allow you to screen for price to book. If the share price is less than the asset value, it's worth taking a good look at the company to see whether you can buy the business at a discount.

Granted, there could be good reasons why the business is trading at such a low valuation - it could be facing onerous debt repayments, it may have a major lawsuit hanging over it, or the assets might be completely without value (for instance, if a manufacturing plant doesn't meet regulations). But quite often, you may find looking at low price-to-book companies can lead you to interesting undervalued sectors and stocks.

2.7 Discounted cash flow valuations

All the other valuation methods we've mentioned are ways of comparing one share with others. Discounted cash flow valuation, on the other hand, can be used to suggest an absolute value for a share, in the absence of any comparatives. However, it does have the disadvantage of requiring quite a lot of work, and you have to be careful to validate your assumptions about future earnings - at the height of the tech boom, analysts were putting together DCF valuations with ridiculously over-optimistic forecasts, and naturally the values those models came up with were way over the top. With those caveats, though, DCF is a really useful way of looking at stocks, and can sometimes spring surprises that can lead you to underrated shares.

The idea behind DCF valuation is *the time value of money*. A dollar you get some time in the future is worth less than a dollar you have in your hand today. If you put $1000 in the bank today and get 2.4% interest, you'll get back $1,024 in a year's time. If you reverse that statement, $1,024 in a year's time is worth $1,000 today. So when we do this valuation, we discount back future expected cash flows to what they are worth today, and then add them together to come up with the value of the business.

You've already learned how to calculate free cash flow. To do a DCF valuation you now need to forecast future years' earnings - usually, a five or ten year projection. Be careful to build some reality checks into the model; it was rumored that one DCF for Facebook included forecast customer numbers in year ten that were slightly larger than the total expected population of the world!

Once you have forecast earnings, you also need to forecast capital expenditure. Will the company need to make a step change at some point? For instance, an extractive company might need to open a new quarry - that's a big all-in-one investment - or an electrical utility might need to open new power stations; it might even have announced its capex plans. You also need to forecast working capital growth - but generally, if you assume it will grow in line with sales, your model should be sufficiently robust.

The next part of the process is to determine the discount rate - quantifying the time value of money. A good place to start is the risk-free rate on government bonds, currently standing around 2.4%, but most analysts also build in a risk premium - because you run more risk buying equities, you need to have a higher reward. Right now, using a discount rate of 5% might be appropriate. (Another approach is to use the company's own weighted average cost of capital, or WACC, which is calculated as the interest rate on its debt plus the required rate of return on its equity. But that's tricky to calculate, and it's different for each company.) A future $100 cash flow has a present value (PV) of $100 \times [1 / (1 + \text{discount rate})^n]$, where n is the number of years between today and the cash payment. So $100 in ten years' time is worth $100 \times [1 / (1 + 0.05)^{10}]$ or about $63. (That's the theory, but unless you were really great at math when you were at school it's probably easier just to use a spreadsheet, to be honest.)

You could also use your required rate of return as the discount rate. If you want to get 8% return on your investments - a feasible but reasonably challenging target - you can build that into the DCF and see what the company is worth that way.

Adding together the value of all future cash flows gives us most of the value of the company. But at the end of the five or ten years, the business should still be worth something, so we need to work out a *terminal value*. There's an academic way of doing this with an equation that assumes the company will keep growing into infinity, but a much easier way is simply to use a PER or EV/EBITDA multiple to get the value at the end of the final year of the forecast period. Don't forget to discount it back to today's value.

Sometimes the results of a DCF can be surprising. Back in the early days of multi-channel television, the UK had only two commercial channels, one of which was highly dominant and had the lion's share of TV advertising. In 1998 ITV was trading as high as 250p a share. That was the year that pay TV firm BSkyB launched its digital channels. Competition soon ate into ITV's advertising revenues. The share price began to collapse, heading below 200p in 2000.

If you listened to many stock market analysts, and if you looked at the PE ratio, you'd have thought the shares would soon recover. However, carrying out a DCF proved interesting. If you built into it an increasing share of viewers for pay-TV channels, revenues fell. (TV ads were priced per thousand viewers, so the fewer viewers, the less ITV received. And if ratings drop, advertising prices are also reduced, further damaging revenues.) At the same time ITV had spent ridiculous amounts of money on a digital channel and on purchasing second-rate sports rights which failed to repay the investment. Assuming that these trends continued for the next five years, the shares were probably worth between 50p and 70p. The DCF was a big warning to get out of the stock. Interestingly, it was also not very far off the company's net asset value of 53p.

It was a good warning. By 2003 the shares were below 75p and heading down - and the analysis also enabled smart investors to get into the stock at relatively low risk towards the bottom, as the company began to get a grip on costs.

2.8 Valuation and a note on "market timing"

You may have heard financial advisers advising clients to avoid "market timing" when the stock market falls dramatically. "Don't sell the market because it's falling! You'll do your portfolio lasting damage!" They advocate what we would call a 100% invested buy-and-hold strategy - buy stocks and then never, ever sell.

We think market timing is dumb, too. If you always buy when the market is racing away, and sell when everyone is panicking, you'll probably be a bit later than the professional investors, so you'll perform slightly worse than the rest of the herd. But if you always look at valuations, you'll probably have hopped out of the market - or at least, you'll be invested in the least exposed and most robust sectors and stocks - before a crash happens. Most downturns happen because market valuations have got way out of sync with reality - so investors who understand valuation are likely to have sold much of their portfolio already, before the bear starts to rampage.

Chapter 3: How good is the company? Performance ratios

Assessing an investment means assessing the quality of the business and looking at the trends that benefit or damage it. But often, discussion is very qualitative and comes down to untested assertions that 'Jeff Bezos is a great manager' or 'Coke is a great product'. Successful investors will do all the reading they can about the business - and that includes looking at trade journals and government or trade body research on the sector, as well as finance papers like Barron's, the Wall Street Journal or Financial times, or websites like Motley Fool or Marketwatch - but they'll also run a whole load of ratios to quantify how well the business is performing.

3.1 Assessing profitability

First of all you want to see how efficient the company is at turning a dollar of sales into a dollar of profit. Different sectors have different characteristics, so a company that's doing well in a low-margin sector might compare badly with a poorly run business in a high-margin trade - make sure you're comparing apples with apples. But it's fair to say that high margins are good, because they give a business more margin for error. If a business is only making 4% on its sales, and one of its cost inputs goes up - for instance, the price of construction materials or raw food ingredients - then it's quite easy for that to push the business into making a loss. If it's making 50% margins, that's much less likely.

High margins compared to competition often show that a company has a competitive advantage. For instance, it may have a much more efficient manufacturing process, or it might have lower real estate costs. In the UK, Wetherspoons established a cost advantage by buying commercial premises such as bank branches that had closed down and turning them into bars - the premises were much cheaper than existing bars and restaurants, and they didn't come with the requirement to buy beer from a particular brewery. That was a competitive advantage that helped the business grow fast. Equally, a good brand or high product quality can enable a business to sell at higher prices, improving margins.

The figures in a company's annual report usually contain a five year run of stats that will let you calculate most of these margins over the longer term. That's really great for spotting trends both in the company, and in the industry as a whole (if you calculate the margins for its major peers). You'll want to ask some pertinent questions though;

- if a company's margins are well below its peers, that could give it room for improvement leading to above-average earnings performance - but does the management have a realistic plan to achieve this?

- If margins have grown consistently, is there still room for more? Or do you think things will plateau?

- Are margin movements linked to a particular trend (e.g. commodity cost reductions, currency movements, or high rental increases) or do they have more to do with company strategy and business quality?

Gross margin

Gross margin is useful when you're dealing with a business which operates as a reseller, for instance a retailer or wholesaler. It's not quite as useful with other styles of company, as typically, labor and indirect costs will have a larger share of the total cost base, though you can still calculate it. To get gross margin you subtract the cost of goods sold from the sales figure, giving you gross profit; then calculate gross profit as a percentage of sales.

Gross margins can have a huge impact on retailers' share prices. Fashion retailers who import their stocks from emerging markets, for instance, can see currency fluctuations take two or three percent off their margin, or might voluntarily give up some gross margin to compete more aggressively. Price wars between US grocers recently saw Kroger report its first quarterly revenue decline in 13 years (in 2016), exacerbated by a 30 basis point reduction in its gross margin. Walmart also saw gross margins fall. That had a huge effect on share prices - Kroger shares dropped from $42 to $23 over two years.

EBIT and EBITDA margins

EBIT and EBITDA margins are simple to work out, taking each profit measure as a percentage of sales. EBITDA is particularly useful for intercompany comparisons, since it gets rid of differing depreciation rates so that you can compare the businesses on a like-for-like basis.

Unlike gross margin, EBIT and EBITDA margins include indirect costs - fixed costs such as premises, head office staff, and maintenance - as well as the direct cost of goods or services. In the case of retailers it's interesting to compare EBIT and gross margin - some retailers score good gross margins, but because they have high real estate costs or have let staff costs grow too fast, don't do so well at EBIT level.

3.2 Returns on Investment

While profit margins are interesting, they don't always show you the whole picture. You need to think about what funds are being used to generate that return, as well. That's why there's another whole family of ratios that use different methods of showing the return on investment - how effectively the company is using its assets.

As with profit margins, you'll want to compare these ratios across the industry to assess any individual company. Usually, better quality companies have better returns on investment than others. But a company with a very low utilization of assets *could* also indicate room for a substantial turnaround - and might flag up a company that's vulnerable to a hostile takeover bid. Ratios are only your tools - it's up to you to interpret them!

Return on Assets (ROA)

Return on assets is particularly useful for asset intensive sectors. Manufacturing companies, for instance, can be judged on whether they manage to use their production capacity to its full extent; though in some cyclical industries, you may see ROA following a wave pattern, as the company invests in new equipment, runs it at a low utilization for a couple of years and then gradually sees it fill up. Businesses that invest in real estate, such as hotels groups, can also be assessed on ROA, though for a true comparison you need to ascertain whether the business actually owns the assets, or leases or manages them - the results in either case will be very different.

ROA includes the current assets as well as the fixed assets of the business, so it's not a bad way to measure retailers' returns - do they turn their stock over fast enough? Are their prices high enough to make up for a lower turnover? IT companies which invest significantly in server farms and data centers, such as cloud computing suppliers, can also be judged by looking at ROA - on the other hand, computing consultancy firms don't have anything like that level of investment, so other ratios are more useful for analyzing their returns.

Return on assets looks at the total assets available to the business, however they are financed. It can be calculated by working out the value of net earnings as a percentage of assets. It's best calculated using the average assets figure for the year, rather than simply the year-end asset number. To get that, usually you can just add the start of year and end of year asset figures together and divide by two, but you can adjust if, for instance, you know that a really big investment was made just before the year end.

ROA shows you how much profit the company made for each dollar invested. Generally speaking, the higher ROA is, the better. But watch out; sometimes, a company has high ROA because it isn't investing in assets for the future. That could be okay for a few years, but eventually it will mean the business falls behind, either with higher costs, or less up-to-date products than its competitors. It's important to look through management statements to get an idea of factors that might affect the ROA -

for instance, a decision to invest in state-of-the-art robotic manufacturing plant might depress ROA in the short term but could be a smart way to achieve market dominance in the longer term.

Return on Equity (ROE) / Return on net assets

Return on Equity takes debt out of the asset valuation and looks at the returns to shareholders, specifically, once debt has been paid off. So it tells you what return you're getting on each dollar of the book value of your shares. (That's *not* the same as the return on the money you actually invested, at market value.) Again, the calculation is simple - net profit as a percentage of shareholders' equity, preferably as a percentage of the average equity during the period.

For some businesses it can be more important than ROA. Banks, for instance, make a tiny return on their assets, which include their customers' deposits

- what's really important is what return they deliver for shareholders.

If you look at a company that's entirely funded by shareholders, the ROE will be the same as the ROA. If it issues debt, then the equity will be lower than the total assets figure - and the ROE, consequently, will be *higher* than the ROA. It can therefore be beneficial for a company to run with a certain level of debt. Be careful, though, of situations where ROE is high because a company has very significant borrowings - good ROE isn't much consolation if the business goes bust due to being unable to pay its creditors.

Return on Invested Capital (ROIC)

Return on Invested Capital is a slightly different twist on the same type of ratio, since it takes net earnings but adds back the interest expense. Because it shows the return on shareholders' funds plus long term borrowings, it shows very effectively how well a company is using its total capital. It uses NOPAT - net operating profit after tax - basically, net income with the interest on debt added back. That has the advantage that you can see the return without needing to take the company's financial structure into account - unlike ROE which is affected by the proportions of debt and equity used to fund operations.

ROIC = (net earnings + interest expense) / (shareholders' funds + long term borrowings)

Activity ratios

Part of the return on capital comes from margins - from the profit and loss account. But the extent to which assets are utilized also has a lot to do with the return - for instance how quickly stocks are turned over and how effectively working capital is used. So you also probably want to look at activity ratios, such as inventory turnover (cost of goods sold / inventory) and days' sales outstanding (receivables/sales x 365), in conjunction with the profit margins we already considered, to show what factors have affected the company's returns.

Inventory turnover is particularly important for retailers, but it can also be crucial to analyzing manufacturing companies. If inventory turnover decreases, that might indicate a number of problems:

- in a fashion retailer, it might show that the business is no longer on-trend - its designs aren't attracting enough customers;
- or it could show that the purchasing department has overestimated demand and bought too much stock,
- or it might show that the business has decided to hang on to some stock for a while rather than reduce prices to try to clear it.

Again, you'll want to look at management statements, as well as at trade journals and business reporting, to try to work out what this number is really telling you.

Days' sales outstanding can also vary for a number of reasons. Sometimes, companies that are taking on large projects are forced to extend longer credit terms in order to win the business. Particularly with big export orders, a deterioration in DSO might actually be the result of good, rather than bad, news. But usually, deteriorating DSO reflects either poor credit control (a source for concern), or deteriorating prospects and profitability in the industry.

3.3 Gearing and debt

Finally, we should mention gearing and debt service ratios. These measure the financial risk of the company you're investing in. As a shareholder, you're one of the very last people to get paid off if a company goes bust, while banks who have lent it money (as well as most bondholders) stand a long way ahead of you in the queue. Over-indebtedness is a major cause of company failure; at the very least, it exposes companies to the risk of having to refinance at disadvantageously high interest rates if market conditions are not favorable when they need to repay debt.

Remember though that debt finance can also be an efficient method of funding for a company, if interest rates are significantly lower than the returns demanded by equity investors. A company that holds significant amounts of cash that aren't used in its operations will have a lower return on capital, because that cash is an asset that's not generating profits.

There are several different ratios to assess debt. The **gearing ratio, or debt to equity ratio**, looks at debt as a percentage of shareholders' funds. Acceptable gearing will differ by industry - generally, sectors with long-term, predictable income streams such as subscription services or real estate companies can sustain a higher level of gearing. As with other ratios, you should make comparisons with other companies in the sector, and with the historic record. If a whole sector has seen gearing increase over the past five years, either it's investing for very significant growth, or returns are not enough to pay for both investment and debt servicing - which could be a warning sign.

While gearing shows the company's financing split on the balance sheet, **interest cover** shows how easily the company can pay its debt service costs. Basically, how many times could the company pay its interest bill out of the operating profit that it's making? It's easy to calculate - EBIT/ interest expense.

An interest cover of 1 would mean the company can only just pay its bankers. That's high risk; just one bad month of sales could mean there's no money to cover interest payments, and bankers could foreclose on the debt. Of course, the company might have cash reserves that it can call on to pay its interest. At 2.5 interest cover, on the other hand, a company has much more margin for error - one bad month won't create problems for the finance director.

Low interest cover also often means a company isn't generating enough cash to pay down its debt - what are known as 'zombie' companies. If a company can't pay down its debt, it may not be able to invest pro-actively in the business, which will eventually dilute its competitive advantage.

Besides the ratios, make sure you look carefully at the description of debt in the financial statements. Debt maturities can be important; a company that is struggling, but doesn't have to repay or refinance debt for the next five years, has time to get its act together, but if debt needs to be repaid at the end of the current financial year, it has a big problem. Financial statements usually show a breakdown of debt by the date repayment is required. Make a note, too, of any loan covenants - these are almost always irrelevant if a company is performing well, but if the value of its assets is reduced (by a real estate crash, for instance, or mark-to-market in the case of banks) or if the company can't meet required ratios due to a collapse in its profits, loan covenants can make the difference.

3.4 Risk / rewards - expected values and scenario analysis

Becoming a successful investor is all about assessing risk and reward. Unfortunately many investors handicap their performance by taking an emotional attitude to risk - "Oh man, that's really risky!" or "this stock is just totally, totally safe, so safe it's boring" - rather than quantifying it so that they can take an education decision. The methods we're going to show you allow you to analyze risk in a disciplined way, which should improve your investment returns significantly.

Quantifying risk

Quantifying risk is something risk managers get to do every day, to work out how much insurance a company needs against potential adverse events, such as a factory fire or a systems outage. To look at a risk we need to think about two things;

1. what's the worst that can happen? But also,

2. what's the chance that it will happen?

Or to put it in mathematical language, we can calculate the severity of a risk as probability x loss. For instance, if we think there's a 50% chance that a company will go from a premium rating to a market rating, as investors reckon it's no longer in the high growth phase, we can work out the impact. At 30 times $4 earnings, the shares are worth $120. At the market rating of 21 times earnings, they're worth $84. The downside is $120-84 = $36. If we think there's a 50% chance of that happening, the risk is $36 x 0.5 = $18. Since reward is just the other side of the risk coin, you can also model the upside in the same way.

Many funds now publish maximum drawdown figures, measuring the fund's greatest fall from peak to trough - the worst that has ever happened. Of course this is historic data, not forecast data, but if we assume that it reflects the nature of the assets in the fund and the way that it's managed, it's probably quite a good way of looking at risk. It enables you to assess the level of risk you're happy with - for instance, you may decide you're not happy with more than 30% maximum drawdown. Equally, you might specify funds with *more* than 15%, as most funds with very low maximum drawdown probably deliver very low returns.

Remember to compare the maximum drawdown with the market, though. If you're looking at maximum drawdown for a tech fund and the history goes back to 1998, you're going to be including a two-year period in which the NASDAQ-100 dropped 78%. A tech fund that only showed 50% maximum drawdown would be pretty low risk in that context, don't you think?

Let's move on to how to use these ratios as a basic scenario analysis. I'm looking at a pharmaceutical company that has one drug on the market, and has just announced a second one in development. The new drug looks really pretty good - it will double net income if it gets through its clinical trials. It might also fail its trials. So I'm going to analyze the expected extra income per share if it succeeds, work out the share price using the upwards-adjusted earnings. I'm also going to guess that the stock will be downgraded if it doesn't, so I'm going to take the expected earnings with just the one drug, but rate the company at 24 times earnings instead of 30.

Next I need to assess how likely the new drug is to succeed. Maybe I put that at just 10%. Because probabilities always add up to 100%, that means there's a 90% change of a downgrade. I can chart the possibilities out in a table:

	New drug succeeds	New drug fails	Expected Value
Net income per share	$20	10	
PE Ratio	30	24	
Expected share price	$600	$240	
Probability	10%	90%	
Expected value	$60	$216	
			$266

Since the share price today is $300 (30 x $10 net income), I'll be a loser if I invest - despite the hype.

You can use this form of analysis to handle any number of scenarios. For instance you might look at the impact of different oil prices on an airline - it will make less money if it has to pay higher fuel prices. You might work out four different profit models, then assess the likelihood of each.

The danger of this kind of analysis is that you can get lost in the numbers. Leave the hundred-tab spreadsheet to the rocket scientists and spreadsheet jockeys of Goldman Sachs or Morgan Stanley. Keep your analysis simple enough that you have a good instinctive grasp of the way it's working out. And remember, although using this approach will help you invest rationally, the model is only as good as the assumptions you've plugged into it.

Chapter 4: Styles of investing

So far, we've given you the tools you need to analyze the market and the investments available to you. If you like, we've given you a piano and we've shown you how the notes are laid out on the keyboard. But just as with a piano, you can play honky-tonk or Mozart, ragtime or Rachmaninoff, there are different styles of investing, Depending on your investment objectives and your personality, you'll probably find one or two are better suited to you than others.

4.1 Contrarian investing

Contrarian investing is basically doing the opposite of what the market does.

That probably sounds like a little boy deciding he hates everyone and he's going to do exactly the reverse of what he's told - not very mature behavior.

But actually, there's a good reason for being a contrarian and it lies in the fact that investors tend to behave like a herd, flocking to invest in the latest fashionable stocks. Very often, that leaves significant investment opportunities in stocks that are unloved, but cheaply valued, or which have growth or recovery prospects that most investors haven't yet noticed.

As Baron Rothschild is supposed to have said, "Buy when there's blood in the streets" - when everyone else is selling, you should be buying, because that's when stocks are cheapest. On the other hands, when everyone is buying, it's time to sell. Some investors like to apply the taxi driver test; when a taxi driver tells you about his latest tech stock tip, place your sell order!

Of course, sometimes a company is lowly rated for a very good reason - its products are trashy, it has the highest costs in its sector, the managing director is a psychopath who believes his own PR, and it's probably going bust on Monday morning, just as soon as the bank it owes money it can't repay gets round to tightening the screws. If you're going to adopt a contrarian approach you really have to do your research. You'll also need enough confidence to stick to your own opinions even if everyone thinks you're crazy. (Personally, I was quite happy when people thought I was crazy to sell my first apartment in the middle of a property boom. I was even happier five years later when I realized how much I would have lost if I'd hung on to it.)

4.2 Value investing

Value investors' great guru is Benjamin Graham. He wrote the book on Value Investing - or rather the books, *Security Analysis* and *The Intelligent Investor* - and they're still available, seventy years later. (They're hard going, but if you really want to follow this style of investing, you really should read them.) Warren Buffett and Charlie Munger, together with

Joel Greenblatt, represent a more recent generation of well known (and high-achieving) value investors.

Value investing is about buying stocks that are undervalued. A stock has an *intrinsic value* based on the quality of its business and earnings, or, in a more traditional economic analysis, the discounted value of all future dividends (remember the DCF model?). What value investors look for is a stock that has been mispriced by the market, so that they can pick it up for less than it's really worth. Value investors are often 'buy and hold' investors - they find a stock that is undervalued and then simply sit on the shares, often using reinvestment of dividends to increase their stake. (However, the best returns come from rigorously reassessing value on a regular basis, and selling stocks which have become overvalued.)

Value investing often goes hand in hand with contrarian investing - in both cases you're looking for value that hasn't been recognized by the market. But contrarians start by looking for unfashionable stocks, then do their research on value; value investors start by looking for lowly rated stocks (screening on PER or PEG ratios, or price to book ratios), which may or may not be contrarian plays.

4.3 Momentum investing

Momentum investing takes a very different approach to the market. There's proof that stocks tend to continue historic outperformance (or underperformance) into future periods. A stock that has outperformed for the past three years is more likely than not to continue to outperform for the next three, for instance. Momentum investors try to make that work in their favor, by buying the stocks that are doing best right now.

Value investors are looking at the *fundamentals* of the companies in which they invest. Momentum investors, on the other hand, ignore fundamentals - instead they look at the behavior of the market. Often, they use share price charts to assist their decisions - this is called *technical analysis*, as opposed to the fundamental analysis carried out by value investors.

However, momentum investors need to be very disciplined to make this style work. It's not just about following trends - if that was the case, you'd end up losing heavily whenever trends reversed. Applying *stop losses* rigorously is the key to making money with this approach; for instance, selling a stock immediately if it falls more than 10% or underperforms the market for two consecutive months. The momentum investor also needs to be happy running a very boring, mechanistic investment process. Value investors can 'buy and hold' and go away on a two or three month vacation; momentum investors need to keep up with the market.

4.4 Growth investing

Growth investors, like value investors, focus on the fundamentals, but they are looking for a different kind of investment. Rather than trying to buy companies which are undervalued, making their returns on the difference between the stock's current value and its intrinsic value, they look for companies which are growing fast, and their returns come from the increase in a stock's share price that accompanies its increasing profits.

If you're willing to get stuck in to doing detailed research, particularly if you have expertise in a growth industry such as IT or biotech, growth investing can be highly rewarding. However, lazy investors following a growth style may find they're on a hiding to nothing; if you follow market tipsters without doing proper research yourself, you'll usually get into stocks well after their growth potential has been priced into the shares. That's not a way to make money - in fact it's a great way to buy into over-hyped shares just before they crash.

Because growth investors are usually buying highly rated shares, they don't benefit from the margin of error that value investors get from buying into shares that trade at a discount to their intrinsic value. That makes disciplines such as diversification and rebalancing (which we talk about in Chapter 6) as well as stop losses extremely important in this style of investing.

4.5 Income investing

Do you remember, right at the start of the book, we talked about the effect of compounding? The longer your money is invested in an asset that delivers an investment return, the more your money grows - as long as you reinvest the returns. That's one reason some stock market veterans believe that income investing is the best way to make above-average returns. Of course, some personal investors are also driven by the desire to use their portfolio to generate an income stream that can help support their lifestyle - that's another reason for income investing.

Income investors look first and foremost at the dividend yield ratio. If a stock doesn't pay a dividend, they're not interested - one reason you don't find a lot of income investors in the tech sector. However, income investing isn't as easy as buying the ten highest yielders in the index. Ideally, you'll focus on companies that may not be paying the very highest yield, but that are expected to grow their earnings - and dividends - strongly in the future. That guarantees a long term income stream and maximizes the effect of compounding. It also makes it likely that the companies' share prices will increase over time.

Buying a very high yield share can be counterproductive if the company is basically liquidating itself - as might be the case, for instance, with a copper mine that only has six years of reserves left. Even if it pays 10% a year yield, at the end of six years you'll have got 60% of your investment back and be left with nothing - you can't call that a successful investment.

4.6 Quantitative approaches

Some investors have developed mechanical investment styles such as 'Dogs of the Dow', a value-based/contrarian mechanism which buys equal stakes in each of the ten highest yielding stocks in the DJIA index. (Because there are 30 stocks in the Dow, this represents the lowest rated one third of the market.) Every year, the portfolio is reassessed, and repositioned with 10% of the portfolio in each of the new 'dogs'.

Other mechanical styles include using stock screening techniques to find, say, those stocks which combine low PER and high return on assets, or the ten stocks on the lowest PEG ratios. While a value or growth investor might use a stock screening technique to find potential investments, they will then carry out detailed research on the companies they have found, using their own judgment. An investor using a quantitative approach will simply buy all the companies that fall into the relevant basket.

Such styles attempt to take advantage of recurrent trends in the market. They have one major advantage in that they remove emotion from the investment process - and emotion is one of the reasons many personal investors underperform. They are also relatively easy to implement, take up little time, don't demand advanced skills in financial analysis, and particularly if used with an annual rebalancing, tend to be low cost.

However, research in 2007 showed the Dow Dogs no longer outperformed. It is possible that adjusting it to focus on NPY (Net Payout Yield - including stock repurchases, which have become a more common way for companies to use their excess cash) can generate good returns, but the change shows that you shouldn't trust a quantitative approach blindly. Try to work out *why* it works, and make sure you check every so often whether it is still working.

Chapter 5: Other equity investments

Investment in shares is hard work. Becoming a successful investor takes time and effort. Unless you're using a mechanical strategy, you'll need to spend time on analyzing financial statements, reading up on industry trends, and keeping up with economics.

But without handing your entire portfolio over to a professional manager, there are some ways you can cut the amount of time you need to spend on your investments. Using a variety of other equity products such as investment funds and ETFs can help you gain a broader exposure to national and international markets, while you concentrate on the direct investments that will really make a difference.

There are also a number of financial instruments that you may be interested in, such as convertibles and preference shares, REITs for exposure to real estate, and a new kid on the block, Peer-to-Peer investment, which you can use to gain exposure to early-stage companies.

5.1 Investment funds

Although there's some evidence suggesting that actively-managed funds struggle to beat the market on anything other than an occasional basis, they do offer a convenient way to diversify your portfolio. For instance, it can be difficult to analyze foreign stocks, and even more difficult to buy them in a cost-effective way, and currency is sometimes an issue, too. By buying funds, you can put investments into emerging markets in order to benefit from the higher growth rates of developing countries, or build a portfolio that reflects global stock market capitalization. and diversifies you away from over-dependence on your domestic market. Or you can use funds to make a bet on a sector which you believe is growing, but in which you simply don't have enough expertise to select your own direct investments (for instance biotech, IT, insurance).

Benchmarking

Almost all funds use benchmarking to some degree. The concept is simple; it's about comparing the fund's holdings to the relevant index. Suppose, for example, that utilities made up 10% of the total market; that's the benchmark, from which the fund can decide to diverge depending on the manager's views of the prospects for the sector. She might *overweight* utilities by putting 11% of the fund into utility stocks, or *underweight* them at 9%. Most funds stay fairly close to the benchmark, though some are more aggressive and a few (often describing themselves as 'unconstrained') don't pay any attention to benchmarks at all.

Benchmarking will tend to keep a fund's performance fairly close to the index; while unconstrained funds can perform much better, they can also, of course, do significantly worse. Ensure you know what kind of bets fund managers have taken in the past, and how they worked out.

Evaluating funds

Choosing which fund to buy can be tricky. However, there are plenty of tools available to help you, including specialized fund website Morningstar.

- Understand the fund's objectives - for instance, it may focus on generating a yield 20% higher than that of the index, or on significant outperformance in terms of capital appreciation.

- Find out the fund's investment style. Is it in line with your style and objectives? For instance, if you're aiming to create a long term income portfolio, investing in a very actively traded hedge fund is probably not a good move. Morningstar is particularly useful here as it shows investment styles in a grid with small to large cap stocks on one axis, and value through to growth investment styles on the other - it's very easy to get a feel for funds from this.

- Big isn't beautiful. Some very large funds find it difficult to continue to achieve outperformance - they're too big to invest in smaller companies, and find it difficult to find enough potential investments to sink their money into. Choose mid-sized funds which are still agile.

- Look at the historical performance figures, but try to understand the reasons for performance. For instance, a fund run by a very active contrarian manager might have really terrible performance for a couple of years if he makes a bad call on one sector - some fund managers were out of technology a couple of years too early. If subsequent performance has been better, the fund might still be worthwhile. On the other hand a fund that has underperformed the market consistently, and is pretty closely benchmarked, has very limited appeal.

Closed-end vs open-end funds

These are two kinds of fund, with different structures.

- Closed end funds ("investment trusts" in the UK) are traded on the stock exchange. Market-makers quote bid and offer prices just as they do with trading companies, and the shares can trade at a premium or (more normally) discount to the underlying net asset value. Just like a normal company, a closed-end fund has a set number of shares in issue - it can issue more through an equity offering, but not otherwise.

- Open ended funds are sold to investors, and bought back from them, by the fund management house, which issues or cancels units as required - so the number of units is always in flux. The 'bid' and 'offer' price are both based on the net asset value of the fund, so you are basically buying at the value of the assets, less the spread.

Because closed end funds can trade at a discount, value-orientated investors can look for funds that are trading at an excessive discount. Should the funds be re-rated, the share price will increase faster than the net asset value giving the investor a geared return. Of course, the downside is geared too. As an example, a fund that is trading at a 19% discount to its $89 net asset value could easily be re-rated to a more normal 8% discount if sentiment towards its sector improves - that would see the share price improve from $72 to $82, a 14% return, even if the net asset value doesn't increase.

Open-ended funds are most appropriate for major markets and sectors where the underlying assets are liquid. However, where they invest in illiquid sectors such as property, if too many investors want to sell out at one time, the fund may have to suspend trading if it does not have enough cash funds to pay out to sellers. This has led to problems, notably during the credit crunch in 2007-8 when numerous real estate funds suspended redemptions. Following the 2016 Brexit referendum vote, three UK real estate funds also had to suspend trading as investors stampeded for the exit.

Remember always to look at the costs of investing in any investment fund. While you shouldn't simply choose a fund on the basis of its cost, the higher the proportion of returns that goes to the fund manager, the less there is left for you.

5.2 Exchange Traded Funds (ETFs)

Exchange Trade Funds work on a different basis from actively managed funds; they mechanically reproduce the performance of an index, tracking its performance (indeed, they're often called 'trackers').

Because their investment process is completely mechanical, they have lower costs than actively managed funds. They trade at asset value less the spread between bid and offer price, like open-ended funds.

ETFs may reproduce a major market index such as the NASDAQ 100, or sectors within the index - for instance there are telecoms and healthcare ETFs. Some are also modeled to provide particular types of stock; for instance there are dividend yield ETFs, growth and value ETFs, or small-cap ETFs.

Some ETFs also enable investors to access non-equity asset classes such as commodities and bonds. Some are geared; that is, they will increase by a factor of the increase in the underlying asset price.

While you might not want to put your whole portfolio into ETFs, they can be useful in enabling you to improve the diversification of your portfolio. For instance, one investor uses ETFs to structure 50% of her portfolio with good exposure to Asia and European stocks, then invests directly in US growth stocks for the remainder. The time and effort she saves using the ETFs can be spent improving her returns on the directly held stocks. There are also inverse ETFs which enable investors to 'go short' and take a bet *against* a market.

The low cost nature of ETFs also makes them a good long term holding; over time, mutual funds' high costs can dilute returns, whereas ETFs are considerably cheaper. ETFs charge under 1% while most mutual funds charge from 1.25% up to 3% of asset value per year.

5.3 REITs

Very few personal investors have enough money to buy commercial property directly. REITs (real estate investment trusts) offer them the chance to acquire shares in a commercial property company and to enjoy the high and stable yield that comes from rental income streams. In most jurisdictions, REITs are obliged to distribute a very high percentage of their taxable income - in the US, 90% - to their shareholders, which ensures they remain high income vehicles.

5.4 Equity/bond mixes

Although most stock market investors buy ordinary shares, there are a couple of special types of investment traded on the exchanges which mix the characteristics of equity and bonds. We're not going to go into great depth of detail here, as the mathematics for analyzing these investments can get very complicated, but they may sometimes be interesting ways to play particular situations. For instance, out-of-the-money convertible bonds can be interesting in recovery situations.

Convertible bonds

Convertibles are bonds which offer a coupon (rate of interest) but can also be 'converted' to equity shares in the issuing company. The bond side offers downside protection, since interest will continue to be paid and if the bond is trading in line with the general bond market, it is unlikely to fall in price; but the conversion rights offer exposure to the equity upside.

Preference shares

Preference shares are part of a company's equity, but behave like bonds - they generally pay a fixed dividend, not one that grows over time. The 'preference' referred to is that given on the liquidation of a company - preference shareholders rank ahead of ordinary shareholders in the order of payout. Preference shareholders are also entitled to be paid their dividends before any dividend can be paid to the ordinary shareholders.

Income investors may find it worth their while investing in preference shares for their steady dividends. It's worth noting that because they are not well understood, preference shares can be undervalued, giving investors a chance to get more income for less money.

5.5 Peer-to-Peer investments

Peer-to-Peer (PTP) investment platforms have proliferated over recent years, giving investors the opportunity to buy shares directly in companies which wish to raise investment capital. Crowdfunding is a godsend for small, innovative companies that don't fit bank lending requirements and are not large enough to secure venture capital.

US crowdfunding platforms SeedInvest and FundersClub were founded in 2012, but until 2016 access was limited to high net worth individuals (accredited investors). From May 2016, crowdfunding in the US has been open to all investors, and the number of portals has increased markedly. In the UK, several PTP investment platforms are now regulated by the Financial Conduct Authority.

While these platforms remain relatively higher risk than the main market, investors who are interested in early-stage companies may find them useful. Most platforms carry out significant due diligence and require companies seeking funding to issue both audited financial statements and an in-depth management discussion of operations.

Chapter 6: Running a portfolio

It's easy to think that good investment is just about finding the right investments. That's very far from the truth. Successful investors know that a lot of their success is down to factors such as diversification, asset allocation, and regular portfolio assessment and rebalancing - the way their individual investments relate to each other, otherwise known as portfolio management. And there's a lot of really boring work that has to be done; regular assessment of the portfolio, checking on the costs of investment, and record keeping. (You may also find that you can greatly increase your investment returns by taking advantage of tax efficient vehicles, particularly if investing in smaller companies.)

In this chapter, we're going to talk you through the basic concepts relating to portfolio management, as well as some of the boring stuff. Compared to an investors who just buy every undervalued stock they see - even if they have quite a good hit rate - smart investors who apply these ideas and manage their portfolios properly will make higher returns over the long term.

6.1 Diversification

Diversification is an investment manager's way of saying "Don't put all your eggs in one basket." By ensuring your portfolio includes different types of asset, or in the case an equity portfolio, stocks that are in different sectors and different countries, you reduce the overall risk you're running.

Investors who had 100% tech-stock portfolios in 2000-2002 got hammered. Investors who had a high percentage of tech stocks, but also had consumer durables, real estate and industrials in the portfolio, suffered much less. Diversification mitigates the harm that any single stock or sector can do to your investments.

However, you do need to think through diversification. For instance, if you buy bonds, housing stocks, and real estate, you might think that's reasonably diversified. In fact, all three investments tend to do badly when interest rates rise, so their returns will be correlated, not diversified. At the same time, you don't necessarily want your portfolio to be totally diversified - you need to be sure that individual investments have the ability to provide you with good returns. That requires striking a balance between betting the bank on one stock (crazily high-risk) and having so many investments that your returns are only around the stock market average. We'd suggest a portfolio of between ten and twenty stocks is plenty.

A diversified portfolio doesn't have to reflect the market. As long as your holdings respond differently to economic changes, you're diversified. For instance, if you hold six growth tech stocks and four high yielding consumer durables stocks, that's pretty good diversification although you don't have any industrials, commodities or banks - because the stocks will tend to perform in different and even opposite ways. (It may not be the best investment strategy, but that's another thing entirely.)

Mutual funds and ETFs can be a good way to ensure your portfolio is diversified. You probably don't have the expertise to invest in emerging markets stocks, even if your broker is able to handle trades in those markets - but you can use funds to give you exposure.

You may also be interested in a couple of rather special cases of diversification. One investor found that whenever she analyzed a sector, she would end up with two stocks that looked attractive. Five times in a row, she chose the wrong one of the two and saw the stock she'd passed on outperform dramatically. Could she solve the problem by making a better choice? Maybe not - but she *could* solve it by buying both the stocks! Another investor not only loved trying to find high performing tech stocks, he was really good at it, but worried that he was over-committed. Since he really didn't find value investing a compelling style, he decided to buy five value-orientated mutual funds as a stable base for his portfolio, and then relied on his tech stocks to provide the hot chili sauce.

6.2 Asset allocation

Most personal investors think of investment in terms of stock-picking - finding individual shares that will outperform. Institutional investors like fund managers and pensions administrators think instead of asset allocation. Their job is to decide what proportion of funds should go into which kind of asset - how much in bonds, how much in equity, and of the equity, how much in property. They use economic and industry data to help them set those targets - then they purchase investments to fill the boxes.

While most of the time you'll be thinking about your equity portfolio as a thing on its own, from time to time you should draw up a balance including all your assets - your home, if you own it, your business, if you're an entrepreneur, and your cash and bond holdings. Look at what major fund houses are saying about asset allocation and see whether your assets reflect that, or whether you're way too much invested in one type of asset. For instance, most people who own their own home are more heavily invested in residential property than they 'should' be according to most ideas of good asset allocation.

You should also look at your portfolio in terms of asset allocation between sectors and geographies - as you need to, if you want to make sure you're adequately diversified.

6.3 Rebalancing and stop losses

You might start out with $5,000 in each of ten stocks, nicely diversified. Each stock represents 10% of the portfolio. But over time, one or two stocks will outperform, one or two will dive, and the others will go along with the market, so that after a couple of years, you have $20,000 in one stock, $10,000 in another, $6,000 or so in most of them, and two that have fallen to only $1,500 each. Your portfolio is now worth $69,000 against your initial $50,000 investment, so you've done pretty well. But your top stock is now worth 29% of your entire portfolio, and your second most successful investment is worth nearly 15% of it. You have 44% of your entire portfolio in just two stocks! And if they're now trading on a premium rating, your risk/reward ratio may have changed dramatically.

That's why we advocate regular portfolio rebalancing. In this case, you'd sell part of your top two holdings to trim them down closer to your original idea of each stock representing 10% of the portfolio. You don't sell the whole holding - you simply reduce its proportion of the total. You might, if you believe the other stocks are all worth investing in, split the proceeds equally to invest a little more in each of your other stakes - and if you think those poorly performing stocks are still a bargain, you might bring them back closer to the original 10% mark.

Rebalancing may mean you miss some gains on your best performers. But it also prevents you ending up as many tech investors did in 2001 - having sat on a portfolio which had seen massive gains on paper, they closed the year with almost nothing.

Stop losses are another way to protect your capital. The way they work is simple; you set the maximum amount that you're prepared to see a stock fall before you sell out. That will differ depending on your appetite for risk, and the type of stock you're investing in; setting a tight stop loss for volatile, high-growth stocks will make you sell out too often, but you probably need a fairly tight stop loss if you're buying turnaround situations that might go wrong. Many investors use a range between 10 and 20%.

Stop losses are a way of recognizing that the market may have information that's not available to you (yet), and that a major price movement downwards could mean there's a profit downgrade coming.

While many traders use stop loss orders with their brokers, investors probably shouldn't - but you should check your portfolio regularly and note whether any stocks have fallen through their stop-loss levels. (You should also reset stop-loss levels occasionally to take account of price movement since your initial purchase.)

6.4 The boring stuff - regular assessment

You need to check your portfolio regularly, and that doesn't mean just looking at the prices on a screen. You need to check

- the balance of your portfolio (which we talked about above)

- recent earnings statements and trends for each stock

- whether all the conditions you originally identified as a reason to buy are stock are still in place - for instance, is it still seeing high revenue growth?

- Whether the stock's valuation has reached levels that make it no longer a value stock, or that you're uncomfortable with.

We'd recommend that you do this at least once a quarter. Set aside a whole day for the process, and make sure you have lots of coffee available!

We'd also advise you to keep an investment diary. Document the research that you do, and any decisions you make, so that later on your can go back and ask 'Why did I invest in this share? What were my expectations? Has it done what I expected?' That way, you can learn from every investment - both successful and unsuccessful. You should also keep documentation on stocks you researched but *didn't* buy. Was your decision right, or did you miss a good opportunity?

Sometimes, the only reason you didn't buy was that the valuation at the time was too high. Keep a watch list of stocks where the underlying business impressed you as fundamentally sound, but the price wasn't right; sometimes, the market will offer you a buying opportunity later on. Plugging your watch list into a portfolio in Google Finance can make good sense - you'll be able to keep an eye on those prices and take action when the stock hits the right level.

6.5 More boring stuff - costs

If you thought quarterly reviews of portfolio performance were boring, we've got even worse - reviewing your investment costs! However, this is one of the best ways for investors to improve their returns. Every time a broker takes a commission or a charges a fee, your capital takes a haircut, and your returns are being diminished.

Costs need to be analyzed in some detail, as many brokers have minimum capital requirements or minimum monthly trades for discounted commission rates. A buy-and-hold investor who only trades a couple of times a year but has a big portfolio will lose out by going with a broker that requires ten trades a month to access the best commission rates. You'll also need to assess the charges for different types of holding - some brokers have very keen prices on stocks but are expensive when it comes to holding mutual funds. It can make sense to have one account for stocks, and another for mutual funds, though this slightly limits your flexibility in moving money between the two.

Whatever decision you make in the first place, you need to keep on the case - brokers keep changing their offers, so what was the best choice five years ago might not be so hot today. For instance, one broker was really competitive until it introduced an inactivity fee for every month without a trade - which might not have been a disaster for frequent traders, but pretty much ruled out the broker as far as less active investors were concerned. Another introduced higher fees on ETFs and mutual funds at the same time as reducing commissions on directly held equity; some investors were much better off, but others with more mixed portfolios suffered.

You also need to think about the frequency with which you trade. Many investors reduce their returns by trading too frequently. Most successful investors are not trigger-happy traders; they make decisive, but relatively few, trades. Some, like buy-and-hold value investors or income investors, will hold stock for the long term, and are most likely to make additional purchases over time, while others have identified the value at which they are prepared to sell, and will wait till that is realized. "Churning" a portfolio to try to catch every small market movement is a sure way to waste money.

Conclusion

If you've read all the way through this book, you may want to get right down to action. Wait a moment! It can be a good exercise to run a paper portfolio for a few months - put your money in some well regarded funds for the moment, and spend some time doing research and making and recording your decisions without actually putting your money at risk. This gives you time to find out your weaknesses before they lose you money. Learning from your mistakes doesn't have to hurt your pocketbook!

By taking the time to read this book, you've acquired all the basic tools that you need to make successful investments. You know how to analyze companies, you know how to value them, you know how markets work, and you know how to run a portfolio. The stock market is full of snake oil salesmen and tempting but flawed investment tips - because you have spent time understanding the basics, you should be able to avoid scams and 'ramping' (where bulletin board posters talk up a share price in order to suck investors into the stock and offload their own stake). You are well equipped to start investing, and whatever your investment objectives, you'll succeed. Markets being what they are, the way might be bumpy - but you already know you should expect some turbulence, and you also know how to protect yourself against it.

Remember that one of the biggest factors that differentiates successful investors is that they understand themselves, as well as the world of investment. They know what style of investment they're good at, and they know what kind of mistakes they're most likely to make - whether they tend to be too optimistic, whether they tend to mistake noise for signal, or whether they don't keep a good check on their asset allocation. Look at your mistakes and work out whether they reflect behavioral mistakes such as confirmation bias or anchoring, or whether you have more to learn about

121

company analysis. You can always learn more as an investor - and the more you learn, the more successful you will be.

You may never become a Warren Buffett or George Soros. That doesn't matter. What matters is that whatever you've defined as your financial objective - whether that's saving for your retirement, making yourself financially independent by the age of 35, or just having some extra income from dividends to make your finances stretch a bit further - you've now acquired the knowledge and skills you need to achieve it.

Resources

The internet is full of great resources for investors, and most of them are free. Here are some of our favorites for educating yourself on the market and the way investors think;

- Berkshire Hathaway reports, investor letters, and presentations. Buffett and Munger are two of the greatest value investors going, and their reports are well written, interesting and highly instructive. www.berkshirehathaway.com

- Morningstar provides in-depth information on mutual funds, including data such as investment style and portfolio breakdown which many finance sites won't show you. Premium services include analysts' reports on funds, which will not only help you make better purchase decisions, but are an interesting way of watching how professional fund managers allocate their investments and what the reasoning is behind their decisions.

- The BlackRock Blog (blackrockblog.com) is a far-ranging blog produced by one of the best rated fund managers, and covering subjects from personal finance issues, through economics and investment themes, to global asset allocation. Add the blog to a feed reader and you'll get a continuous stream of provoking content.

You'll also want resources for valuing stocks and finding companies' financial statements.

- Stock exchanges' websites are a good place to start for finding share prices and company filings. The New York Stock Exchange (www.nyse.com), NASDAQ (www.nasdaq.com) and the London Stock Exchange (www.londonstockexchange.com) all offer huge amounts of data.

- Marketwatch (www.marketwatch.com) not only has stock market news, but also has a huge database of company financials, including analyst estimates for many stocks.

- Motley Fool (fool.com) is a well regarded website for individual investors, with newsletters, forums, and a number of paid-for services. It's a site that focuses on the fundamentals, so if you're a value or growth investor and want to talk about your favorite stocks with others, it's a great community. (However, UK based investors should note the UK discussion boards have now closed down.)

- Yahoo Finance (finance.yahoo.com) allows you to build a portfolio and follow your stocks online, giving news updates as well as share prices and financial stats. There's also an app for iTunes users which provides live updates.

- Don't forget companies' own websites, which often include detailed presentations given to analysts and recordings of the analysts' conference calls, as well as SEC filings.

Disclaimer

The information contained in **"Stock Market Investing for Beginners"** and its components, is meant to serve as a comprehensive collection of strategies that the author of this eBook has done research about. Summaries, strategies, tips and tricks are only recommendations by the author, and reading this eBook will not guarantee that one's results will exactly mirror the author's results.

The author of this Ebook has made all reasonable efforts to provide current and accurate information for the readers of this eBook. The author and its associates will not be held liable for any unintentional errors or omissions that may be found.

The material in the Ebook may include information by third parties. Third party materials comprise of opinions expressed by their owners. As such, the

whole or in parts. No parts of this report may be reproduced or retransmitted in any forms whatsoever without the written expressed and signed permission from the author.

www.ingramcontent.com/pod-product-compliance
Lightning Source LLC
Chambersburg PA
CBHW070352220526
45467CB00001B/344